SOFTLY WAKES THE D[...]

An East Anglian Year of Nature

by

Hugh Brandon-Cox

BOOKS BY THE AUTHOR

Wanderings with the Woodman	Thames Publishing, London
Trail of the Arctic Nomads	Wm. Kimber, London
Summer of a Million Wings	David and Charles, Devon
Hovran (Swedish Bird Lake)	Tidens, Stockholm
Lure of the Wilderness	East Countryman
Mud on my Boots	East Countryman

Published by
Grice Chapman Publishing
The Shire House, Burgh next Aylsham
Norwich, NR11 6TP

www.gricechapman.com

© Hugh Brandon-Cox 2003
All paintings and photography by Hugh Brandon-Cox

ISBN 0-9545726-3-7

Designed and printed in England by
Barnwell's Print Ltd, Barnwell's Printing Works
Penfold Street, Aylsham, Norfolk, NR11 6ET
Telephone: +44 (0)1263 732767

HUGH BRANDON-COX

Foreword

We live today in a world that is changing so much because of the tensions between the nations that it becomes a huge relief to turn to the wonders of the great world of nature.

I was sent as a small boy into this world; into the hedgerows and the saltmarshes, and my charming old grandmother started me on a journey of discovery that has never ended.

My book *Mud on my Boots* has shown me, by all the letters I have received, that to try to depict something of the enormous beauty of the natural world is very much welcome. So I sincerely hope that *Softly Wakes the Dawn* will give much pleasure to all who need it and enjoy the illustrations of a year in East Anglia's nature.

My sincere thanks must go to the great help I have received from Susan Grice, who has gathered the material I have written for the *Suffolk Norfolk Life Magazine* month by month over several years, to form the chapters of this book.

Also I must thank the Barnwell's team of printers for the manner they have worked to achieve such a high standard of perfection in the whole presentation of my work. There are so many others who have urged me to complete the book, despite a long illness. If any readers would like to write to me with their views I will always be delighted.

Go out and marvel at the smallest creature you can find. Each is a miracle of life and beauty.

Hugh Brandon-Cox

Tall Chimneys
Bessingham
Norwich
Norfolk NR11 7JR
Tel: 01263 577777

Right: *Grey Heron in the dawn. Sights like this are rare and must be a delight for all time.*

January

The first rays of the light of a new dawn reach through my window and touch the wall near my head. In the distance comes the muffled crowing of a cock. It is the start of a January day. The light is reluctant to brighten. A heavy mist has lain over the sodden ground all night and now, as the low sun tries to break through the thick pale grey haze, the rural scene around my cottage in the very heart of Norfolk has an air of mystery.

January can vary enormously. Often it is very mild and a few flowers can be seen in the fields where the winter wheat is already green. It can be desolate and cold, but to our coastline thousands upon thousands of migrating birds sweep in from distant breeding sites - Siberia, Greenland, Iceland, Scandinavia and even Canada.

There is no more thrilling sight on a bleak cold day than to watch a huge flock of pinkfeet geese wheeling and calling high overhead above the great fields around Brancaster. They settle in a mass of large noisy birds onto the ground that only a short time ago was thick with sugarbeet. They have come to feed on the tops left after the harvest.

I find myself drawn more and more to the great sheet of mud and sand flats that we call the Wash. This is the second largest area of inter-tidal land in the British Isles. More than a quarter of a million birds from a colder north make this paradise of mud their home for the winter, finding food for each type of probing bill. This was once the happy hunting ground of the wild-fowlers with their long punt guns, but now it is protected, and the guns are heard no more.

There is a great charm about the ebb-tide when the small pools left as the tide recedes are full of creatures belonging to the minute world, and the smell of the saltings and the mud is strong in the nostrils. As the tide begins its rapid return, gurgling as it swiftly flows up the small creeks that cover the surface, so the mass of waders that have been scattered over the vast area are forced further inland and eventually they come within sight in a great variety of flashing wings and noisy calls. It is an exciting time and one forgets the chill wind in the thrill of watching knot and dunlin, turnstones, ringed plovers, redshanks, bar-tailed godwits, little white sanderlings, and the yelping large oystercatchers, as they are compelled to sweep in to the very shoreline. Often they will then settle for several hours to await the welcome return of their precious mud which contains the food to sustain them all winter. At times one can see the lovely little snow buntings. I have filmed them at their nests in North Norway.

The great salt marshes of the coast have been formed through the centuries by a mixture of silt, clay and sand, creating a muddy bed that is colonised by a host of sea-tolerant plants. Through the years this area has become

Right: The rural scene in winter

HUGH BRANDON-COX

Coming from Scandinavia for the winter, small flocks of snow buntings can be seen on the coast.

Oystercatchers on a winter morning.

immensely important to wild life. As the countryside becomes ever more broken up by roads, new housing estates and all the impediments of modern living, so the areas where it is still possible to gaze out at a big expanse of sand, sea and sky become an increasingly treasured possession.

Survival in the wilds

All creatures from the smallest insect to the largest mammal or bird have adapted to cope with the seasons. In our own country three creatures that survive by hibernation are the hedgehog, dormouse and the bat, modifying their lifestyle to a state of suspended life throughout the winter months. We have other cold-blooded creatures such as snakes, frogs and snails that become torpid in winter but it is only the warm-blooded creatures that change their habit and body temperature in tune with the air around them. Hibernation is usually thought of as a very deep sleep but it is really much more than that. The heartbeat slows and breathing almost stops, and the temperature of the body falls to within two degrees of freezing. These changes mean that they use up only a tiny amount of energy to maintain their life. In hibernation the whole mechanism of the body just ticks over and the animal lies almost dead to the touch, stiff and cold.

The dormouse chooses the bottom of a hedge or the foot of a coppiced hazel, and hedgehogs may use an old burrow. They all build with dead leaves a warm nest among old logs or even under a shed. These nests form an insulating layer and keep the temperature up to about five degrees Celsius most of the time. This is the best temperature for hedgehogs to hibernate efficiently and so long as they are protected from snow and frost for three or four months they will remain in this suspended state, totally unaware of what is going on around.

All hibernating mammals need to eat particularly well before their period of inactivity in order to live on the fat they store in their bodies. Hedgehogs and bats cannot store nuts and seeds so they must keep a whole winter's energy requirements in their own bodies in the form of white fat. It accumulates under the skin and around the body in the autumn and by the time winter comes this fat can account for up to a third of the animal's total weight.

We have some 16 species of bats in the British Isles and most of them are solitary in their hibernation, although some do winter in groups. A cellar, a hollow tree, or a cave are places with a relatively constant temperature and high humidity which reduce the danger of the bats losing water by evaporation. Old mines and large roof spaces, such as in barns and attics are good spaces too. The big horseshoe bat hangs upside-down from the roof of a cave, while the 'daubenton bat' squeezes itself into narrow crevices or will even burrow among loose material on the cave floor. Bats are particularly sensitive to disturbance and, if aroused, their chances of survival are greatly reduced, so cave searchers should take care.

One would think that waking up would be quite a simple affair - but it is not. The hedgehog or the dormouse has to raise its temperature through some 30 degrees. This is achieved by using a special tissue called brown fat whose only purpose is to generate heat to warm the circulation around the body. I have watched a young hedgehog coming round from a winter's sleep and when its muscles were warm enough it began to shiver and stretch its limbs in the most human looking manner, producing more heat as it did so. A bat may take fully half an hour to rouse itself but a hedgehog can take twice as long, even on a sunny day.

Hibernating animals cannot defend themselves against predators so during the winter months it is quite possible that between 30 per cent and 60 per cent of hedgehogs and bats never live to see their next spring.

Herons suffer badly if the pools are frozen.
Flight of pinkfeet geese.

Winter wings

On a normal country walk along the hedgerows and lanes these days one sees very little of wildlife. A pair of beautifully coloured jays, viciously bad tempered, call abuse with a voice like a piece of ripping calico. They have a great dislike of humans. Rooks wheel around in the air, their screeches vibrating through the still, frosty day. They are a bad tempered gang as they settle for the night on the top-most twigs of the tall trees. Dragging their ragged black feathers around their gaunt bodies, they have nothing to be pleased about, it seems, as they disturb the gathering dusk.

The old grey heron, which has been in every pool and lakeside all through the summer, now finds one morning that his strong beak will not penetrate the thick ice that has covered his favourite haunt. He knows by instinct that if he doesn't find food quickly he will die. So he opens his broad, wide grey wings and makes for the coast, to the estuaries and open places where he will try to catch small fish from the sea.

Bands of coots, which have hated each other all spring and summer, now gather in flocks and head in the same direction. They mingle with brent geese on the estuaries and mud flats. Even the very attractive little kingfisher deserts its haunts along the riverbanks and heads for the estuary when the river can no longer provide a source of food in very hard weather.

In some winters the handsome waxwing comes to visit in great numbers. If you have visited the lovely dunes at Holme in Norfolk, you may have seen this little bird on sea buckthorn, the berries of which are a bright orange and greatly loved by the waxwings. It is rare that you will see one alone, they prefer to stay in groups.

If you want to see huge flocks of lapwings, the Buckingham Marshes near Strumpshaw Fen Reserve in

The wigeon are certainly one of the handsomest ducks that come into Norfolk & Suffolk each early spring. They leave here about September or later.

Norfolk is the place to go. As a small boy, and still today, I have always found the cry of the lapwing very mournful and melancholy. As it sweeps over the fields close to its nest, it calls 'pee-wit, pee-wit' as though already mourning the fate that so often befalls it. Many of the early nests are run over by the tractors. It was estimated some time ago that we had about 180,000 pairs of lapwing breeding in this country. They are very good friends to the farmer. It is a real joy on a lovely winter day to see huge flocks wheeling about in the sky.

The wigeon is another really beautiful marshland bird, and companion to the lapwing. Although in Britain this lovely bird rarely exceeds 500 breeding pairs, in winter they come from Northern Europe, Iceland and Russia and as many as 200,000 are thought to be present during the January peak period. The most evocative sound of a salt-marsh is certainly the soft whistle of the male wigeon as they rise in big groups and the sunlight reveals their lovely colouring. The wigeon is about the size, and somewhat like, a mallard with a short neck and tiny bill. If you watch a flock grazing, you see the birds diligently plodding through the grass, pulling it up and cropping quite large areas very effectively. When they rise their call and the prominent white patch on the upper wing of the male are distinguishing features.

Can there be a more charming bird to be seen in January on the seeds of the willow herb, burdock or thistle head than the handsome little goldfinch? I think not. To see a pair with that lovely yellow wing - bars and heads of deep red, twittering with notes that remind one of a world of Japanese gardens, is to experience a warm thrill that will last all of a cold day. When the trees and hedgerows are in full leaf again in May, a pair will build a soft rounded nest, often in the fork of a fruit tree. Small twigs, many soft grasses and lichens will form the nest.

Whatever the weather the blackbird is always there.

Lovely in colouring, waxwings also come to our region in winter.

11

February

This can be the most bleak and cold month of the year. There is a viciousness about the wind, especially if one is on the Norfolk or Suffolk coast. There is very little life to be seen in the fields but, nonetheless, a feeling that spring will emerge before long.

Coastal reflections

With grim, relentless fury the winds stung my face, smarted my eyes. Howling direct from the cold steppes of Siberia, it reached the open mud-scape at Brancaster with low, moaning anger. Snow had begun to fall and the sky was deepest blue-grey. I began to retrace the deep mud-gripped footprints I had left as I plodded out to the distant horizon. I reached the shelter of a long line of sand dunes held fast by the tough marram grass. Thin mists of sand wound through the waving grasses and I made for the bottom of a deep dune. A mass of driftwood had been thrown up by a winter gale. I drew from my old leather rucksack a battered kettle and army heater and soon had water boiling for some very hot tea. As I gazed into the sky I wished for a companion to talk of books, of people, of geese passing overhead, of the approaching night sky.

I sat too long on this February afternoon. The cold had crept into my bones. A passing red shank yelled his alarm call as he swept over on swift beating wings. My mind went back to the time when Norfolk was still united to the continent. The great North Sea basin was a land of forests and swamps and fresh water pools before it was inundated with salt water around 6400 BC. At several places on the North Norfolk coast, as at Titchwell, the trunks and stems of ancient trees can still be seen at low tide.

My way back to Brancaster Staithe was guided by the yellow lights of the brick and flint houses, strongly built to withstand the north winds. I gazed back and could hear, gradually and then more urgently, the wind gurgling in the creeks as the tide swept in to flood. The influence of the tides and the sea has always had a great effect on the whole region. In 1565, it was noted for Customs, Hunstanton, Heacham, Wells, Thornham, Burnham, Brancaster, Blakeney, Wiveton, Cley and Salthouse were thriving ports. It was one of England's busiest trading coastlines. But the movement of great sand banks has resulted in the silting up of the shipping channels, though Wells's ancient quay can still take fair-sized vessels. I remember standing near the pine trees at Wells with the weather so cold that even the ebb tide estuaries had a sheen of cracking ice on the shallow pools of the mudflats. In the fields, greylag geese could be glimpsed through a thin vale of mist. On snow covered banks by the channel, a large flock of brent geese had gathered, their dark bodies contrasting with the winter scene around. Groups of coots coming from frozen inland lakes wandered miserably over the snow and a couple of grey herons huddled into their large wings.

Right: *February sunset*

February is usually the coldest month of the year.
Sheep in the snow on a gloomy day.

A changing world

Small farming is a tough life nowadays. Talking to two brothers who farm in my north Norfolk village of Bessingham, I learn that 138 acres is not enough to provide a living. One brother has to be a book-keeper to a large concern four days a week and the other, during the summer at any rate, turns his hand to fencing, painting, gardening, hedging and decorating to supplement their income. Their story is the story of today's small farmer. They rely almost entirely on grants for set-aside land and the arable crops they grow. The simple routines that were a way of life a few years ago are now replaced with red tape. New laws, for example, make it difficult to dispose of sheep dip liquid onto the fields where it always went. So the sheer effort and cost of keeping sheep has forced the brothers out of sheep farming.

As soon as the earth is turned by the tractors, it is a signal for every gull in the area to come down and search for grubs behind the plough. But whereas the ploughing used to be in the early spring, it is now mostly in the autumn, almost as soon as the other crop is cleared from the field. The great army of lapwings that used to patrol across the fields performing a very useful service to the farmer by consuming the grubs seem to have almost disappeared - another sign of our declining bird population. The stubble fields provided both food and shelter for many birds, especially the partridges. Insects were there in abundance. Now it is rare to see a family group of these birds flying low over the brown ploughed, extended fields. Where once wide headlands provided shelter and food for birds and animals, the fields are now often ploughed to the very edge.

Melancholy cry

The mournful cry of the lapwing as it wheels and sweeps over the fields is a familiar sound in February. As they tumble and twist, crying 'pee-wit, pee-wit', they appear to be worried for good reason. These attractive birds, with a crested head, are a lovely deep bottle green with a purple sheen. They make almost no nest but scrape a dip in the grass very early in the year. Just as the eggs are laid, the plough comes along - though less in these days of autumn ploughing - and they will have to start over again.

The lapwing, though classed among the wading birds, has a very short beak which is not suited for the mud at all, but rather for the damp grassland that they frequent in the winter. It is in the coldest days of the month, when the fields are too hard too penetrate for grubs and insects, that the lapwings turn to the coast. The lapwing will breed in a large number of habitats as long as they have patches of short grass or bare ground suitable for feeding. Most breeding birds are found on marginal land, often around pits or quarries. But I always feel that they are really a farmland bird and it is there where I have watched them and, as a boy, plotted to discover their nests.

Ground nesting birds such as the 'Pee-wit' have many enemies to contend with. Magpies, crows and foxes are predators, but the lapwing will defend its young vigorously. When they tumble down on their enemy, their wings make a great swishing noise - usually enough to put off the intending predator and leave the eggs unharmed. For the nest, the male bird makes several scrapes in the ground using his feet and then lines it with dry grass. Along comes a female and chooses one of them in which to lay a clutch of four eggs, stone-coloured with black blotches which camouflage them beautifully. Arranged with their points facing inwards, the eggs make a neat square. The young hatch with a covering of down and with their eyes open. As soon as they dry out they are able to get around the nest and even to feed themselves under the watchful eye of the adults.

It takes about five weeks for the chicks to fledge and the parents have to defend them all this time - often with great difficulty if there are sheep in the field. After the breeding season the birds disperse over a wide area, often

The mournful cry from the welcome lapwings. The eggs are beautifully coloured, but easily broken by tractors.

15

breeding as far away as Central Europe in the following year. They are great nomadic wanderers, and their numbers depend very greatly on the weather. Any really cold spell is usually heralded by big flocks of lapwings such as I have seen in Norfolk fields. They will be heading west or south again in the hopes of finding warmer weather. But when the thaw sets in, we find them back again.

High in the trees

The rooks are probably the first to set up a home again. They are around our fields in big noisy flocks, and spend time grubbing away in the near-frozen fields. They are doing more good than harm, unlike the pigeons who do considerable damage to whole fields of crops. It always amazes me that birds like the rooks wish to start rebuilding their nests in such remarkably cold conditions. As the evenings approach they sit like sorrowing miners' widows, with wing feathers dragged round them like black shawls. They do not like the dark or the cold but they survive, and very quickly they have youngsters in their high twig nests.

In the garden one can sometimes see the cheerful little figure of the wren. Too small and delicate, it seems, to combat the winter. But they have several ways of surviving. Several will band together and occupy either a hole in a tree or a nest box and huddle together for warmth during the night. The ivy, a remarkably thick plant, gives them good shelter during the dark hours.

This is the time when the first lambs are born and they need all the protection they can get. Mostly, they have hay bales, and are sometimes kept indoors. The old shepherds that I used to know had small huts on wheels where they lived for some time during the long lambing season. They were totally devoted to their flocks of sheep and home life waited until the lambing was over.

Rooks high in the trees.

Sheep have always played a big part in East Anglia and I often frequent the area of flat land around Horsey, with its very fine old drainage mill. Here you can see sheep grazing as they have done through the centuries with very little change. Here and all the way along the coast great flights of pinkfeet geese will pass over. All through the winter days we have watched them and listened because they have one of the most thrilling calls of nature. Before long they will begin to make their way back to the tundra regions where they nest.

The frog's courtship

It is during February that the frogs begin to waken from their winter torpor, and they are to be found in stagnant ponds and ditches. They always seem to be drawn to still water. On a quiet day you can hear the males croaking and the larger females calling back with deep grunts. In the courtship, the male will grab any female available and, with his sucker pods, attach himself to her back and remain there. The mass of foaming eggs will be spawned in March and early April and hatch during May into the tadpoles so beloved by small boys.

Frog spawn was once used as a poultice to stop bleeding and we are told that effective cures were made by 'binding yee green fome where frogies have the spawn'. In old times, the word tadpole came from a word meaning toad-head and these tadpoles were once eaten in the belief that they cured gout. Tadpoles are the major food source for many fish, newts and water birds. Only a few of the great number that are spawned each year survive to emerge as small adults in mid-July.

The month of February can be all things to all men. It stands on the very edge of a new spring. There is always something to see, even in this coldest month.

Marsh tits come to the willows and hazels.

Rooks nest very early in the tallest trees.

March

I am standing in the walled garden of a very old house in the stillness of a quiet March morning. From an open window comes a beautiful deep contralto voice singing Softly Wakes My Heart, from Samson and Delilah. I am transfixed to the spot, listening to these lovely sounds and conscious of the beauty of the morning.

The notes fade and there is silence for just a moment. Then, from the top of the tallest tree beside me comes another beautiful sound: the clarion notes of a cock blackbird. Clear and melodious, the bird takes up almost the refrain to which I have been listening.

The blackbird has a mate and already there is a nest with eggs in a nearby bush. The world of nature has begun its annual pursuit of life. Every bird has its own peculiar song, in some very feeble and in others - as the blackbird and the nightingale - glorious. Then there is the tiny wren, with its shattering displays of noise and bustle; the soft cooing of the turtle dove and the raucous screaming of the rook. They all have their place in the symphony of nature's great orchestra, all proclaiming once again that spring is coming.

The beauty of early flowers

Since January we have seen the gradual awakening of the early spring flowers. Go into the woodland on a crisp March day and what will you find? There is, if you are lucky, a smattering of lovely white wood anemones, looking for all the world like snowflakes. I have a great affection for these flowers, with their creamy blooms flecked with pink and giving off an odour something like leaf mould. The flowers droop at night and during damp weather and come alive when the sun returns.

Then, in wetter ground, you may find the lovely marsh marigold, with its splendid big yellow head, a true native of these Isles which was here long before the Ice Age. It is one of the brightest and most cheerful flowers at this time, often lasting through to May or early June. The marsh marigold contains a poisonous substance which gives the foliage a sharp taste and if it comes into contact with the skin it can cause blistering. Nevertheless, the Saxons would apply the leaves of the marigold to boils as a counter irritant.

Beneath the spring primroses you will find ground ivy, often overlooked because it has no semblance of the leaves of normal ivy and grows prostrate on the ground. But it covers the earth with a beautiful little purple flower at this time of year. It is, in fact, a member of the mint family and deters animals from grazing upon its foliage by emitting a spicy aroma.

Right: *The grey partridge has declined so much recently.*

HUGH BRANDON-COX

In the past, ground ivy was used by brewers to clear the ale and give the brew a strong, bitter flavour. It was known by the name 'alehoof' by the Saxons and remained the major flavourant used in brewing until the 16th century when the cultivated hop was introduced. In Georgian England this small plant was believed to be a good treatment for the damaged eye of cocks injured in fighting. It was said that the owner of a cock chewed a few leaves, sucked out the juice and spat the saliva into the bird's damaged eye. And ground ivy used to make a herbal remedy called gill tea with a mixture of honey, sugar, boiling water and ivy leaves. It was claimed to help those suffering coughs and colds.

The Hare and the Partridge

In my mind the hare and the grey partridge symbolise the countryside in March in many ways. This is the month when the so-called Mad March Hares display their mating and fighting qualities to the best. But today the sight of these confrontations is becoming rarer. We do still have a fair number; they are not so destroyed as they used to be by shooting. For most of the year the male hare lives alone but during March they gather together in open fields to perform their antics, a strict ritual of boxing and bucking. The effect is to impress a female and to drive away rivals. The hare's hind legs are extremely strong and if they hit a rival you can hear a scream like a newborn baby.

Hares try to remain quite motionless during most of the day, depending for camouflage on their russet coat which blends beautifully into the surroundings. They emerge at twilight to feed upon bark, roots, grass and all produce of arable fields. When they run there is no more agile an animal as it bucks and weaves across the fields into the distance. If it is possible, a hare will always try to run up-hill because his long back legs are several inches longer

March is the time the lovely wood anemones start blooming.

than the fore limbs, giving it an advantage over, say, a fox. Back in Norman times, the hare was considered by the nobility to be well worthy of the chase. It had the honour of being one of the four beast of venery, alongside the deer, boar and wolf, which were all wild in our land at that time.

A similar story applies to the partridge, whose population in England has reduced by 75 per cent since the Second World War. This is a pattern repeated all over Europe. The intensive use of chemicals in farming and the loss of hedgerows are the main culprits. It has been suggested that farmers should leave headlands sown with wild seed mixtures and stubble fields unploughed through the winter, leaving a haven for the partridge, hare and many other forms of wildlife.

Arrivals and departures

Now is the time that the first of the small birds from Africa arrive in our hedgerows, which are covered white with blackthorn blossom. From our shores millions of birds have gone back, or are preparing to go to warmer climes in Africa and other regions where they have their breeding grounds. It resembles a railway junction of movement, in and out of the country.

We are fortunate in our garden to have a little group of sparrows all the year around. In the winter they are very busy in the bushes, chirping away, and managing to satisfy themselves in a way only done if there is a group together. All the small birds that have been in great flocks all winter are now splitting up to perform the function for which they have been born; that is, to reproduce, to find a suitable place for nesting, to lay their eggs, to feed the youngsters on whatever food is available. All this so that they may survive, to make sure that next season there is another selection of tiny wrens, robins, thrushes or willow warblers to carry on the breed.

March hare

Partridges in flight

21

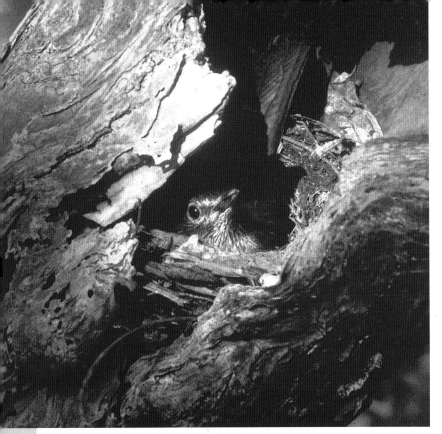

The Winter Hedgerow

We have an enormous number of hawthorn hedges in England. With its spiny twigs, it is very difficult to break through, certainly by humans. They were planted to contain livestock and also to give shelter from the fierce winds of winter. Many birds roost in the hedge overnight and the small hawthorn thicket may accommodate hundreds of starlings and large flocks of fieldfares, stock doves, wood pigeons and even magpies. The hedge offers them good protection, especially from the strong northerly wind, which can break down the resistance of even the hardiest birds during long winter nights.

The hedge is also a very attractive repository for food in the winter because a mature hedgerow offers quite a large range of foodstuffs. Blackbirds, thrushes, starlings, finches, sparrows, tits, fieldfares and redwings all enjoy the profusion of berries and seeds, especially the berries of the ivy. They are not very nutritious but they go like all the rest, as do the fruits of the spindle, honeysuckle and briony. Also in winter the mice, squirrels and voles bury seeds and nuts. Wood mice and bank voles, being good climbers, are able to get at the berries that grow high up in the hedges. A typical menu in winter would include rosehips, haw berries, hazelnuts and acorns. The wood mice eat only the hard centre of the haws, discarding the fleshy coat, whilst the bank voles will do exactly the opposite.

All this food means that quite a number of animals can remain active throughout the year. But little killers like the weasels and the stoats have to be very versatile to survive a severe winter. These predators have to alter their diet, sometimes even including roosting birds if they can catch them, and search the fields for whatever food can be picked up. Even the large badgers will come out of their sets at night and trample about in the mud or snow to find food.

Blackbirds nest early and sometimes choose hollow trees.
The redwing, which comes over from Scandinavia for the winter.

In an old country lane lined with hedgerows, you can find ash, hazel, oak, holly, spindle, hawthorn, blackthorn, ivy, brambles, dog roses and honeysuckle all intermixed into a wonderful variety of useful and edible products. Throughout the whole year the hedge is a haven to a whole host of small mammals, birds and plants. As our hedgerows have declined so drastically, with huge agricultural machines requiring great fields to be economic, hedgerows have been rooted up and spraying of insecticides has greatly reduced the number of helpful insects that provided a variety of food for birds such as the partridge. The young of such birds rely greatly on the small caterpillars, which are about in great numbers at the time when they are very young. It is a tragic irony of fate that we destroy so much in order to create a greater yield of crops, only to have the farmer ordered to set aside these fields.

Almost every hedgerow tree and shrub has a special use. The hard wood of the hornbeam was used for machine cogs; the hawthorn for rake tines, and the pale wood of the holly and maple for turnery. Dogwood and spindle make skewers; the blackthorn is crafted into walking sticks and the elder for millions of pegs, which the gypsies used to sell at our doors.

The rural scene we try to preserve for as long as possible.
The handsome cock pheasant and duller hen fly about the primroses.

Walk along the hedgerows and look at them as you have never looked before. Think of what they have sustained over the centuries. Even today, hedgerows have a vital role. Long may the pheasant be able to lay its eggs in safety and, we hope, the partridge may come back from its decline.

March is a month when you can go out and see a great deal happening. Look carefully. The reward of watching what there is day by day will far outweigh the bitter winds that we sometimes have to endure.

April

On a blustery April day, the trees outside my house are swaying in the wind. The rooks are viciously shouting. They are amongst the earliest birds to nest and choose the top of the tallest trees, as do the grey heron. For other birds, this month is one of great coming and going.

The geese and the waders will be leaving for their summer nesting grounds. To our shores come the army of migrants, mostly small birds like the warblers, to add to the music of the woods, fields and marshes.

The robin is a favourite of the British people, with a song for every season. In the spring it is full of joy and enthusiasm. In the autumn it sounds so very sad. The song thrush has a beautiful call. Listen to its long message and pick out the distinctive sounds: 'stick-to-it, stick-to-it', 'you'll-do-it, you'll-do-it'. The blackbird has a very melodious voice and sings very early in the year. The lovely little willow warbler has one of the most charming songs of all. It starts on a high note and then descends, almost as though it were imitating the skylark. Its little nest is hidden away in the grass and carefully guarded.

Perhaps the two birds that we most love to hear are the nightingale and the skylark. The skylark has inspired a great many poets, writers and musicians. What a great pity it is becoming increasingly scarce these days. Wandering along the edge of a salt marsh, in Norfolk or Suffolk, one hears the lovely outpouring of this courageous bird as it heads higher and higher into the sky, finally becoming invisible to the eye. But its sound does not diminish. I am reminded of the insistent, lyrical melody of Vaughan Williams' *The Lark Ascending*. And what bird could not be greatly liked that sings, as the nightingale does, throughout the short summer nights.

Seldom seen but often heard

Eagerly awaited every year is the notorious, echoing call of the cuckoo. In the past, cuckoo fairs were held on 14th April to celebrate the return of this migrant because it was thought that they were bringing back the warm weather. The cuckoo is widely distributed throughout Britain and is quietly attractive when you see it. But it is seldom seen, although its distinctive call gives the feeling of it being all around. It has a slate blue body with black and white bars on the under side. During its period with us it feeds on spiders, worms, caterpillars and even the larva of the tiger moth, which is poisonous to other birds.

The cuckoo is not a bird that we can really like. It never builds a nest of its own but instead lays its egg into the unsuspecting nest of a much smaller bird. The female will repeat this laying until she has laid about twelve eggs in different nests, so that there is a certainty that the cuckoo population never goes down. It has very good eye sight

Right: There is a great charm as the fresh leaves appear.

HUGH BRANDON-COX

and will select in advance the kind of bird to foster its young: it might be a meadow pipit, a hedge sparrow or quite often it is the lovely little nest of the reed warbler in the reeds. The eggs will hatch in about thirteen days and the youngster is strong enough to push the true young of the foster mother out of the nest. Within three weeks, the intruder's weight has increased many times. Although it has no parents to teach it, by autumn the young bird is ready to migrate. With uncanny skill, it sets off towards winter quarters in Africa and the Middle East, covering thousands of miles.

A nocturnal friend

April is the month when it can be fascinating to watch the newly emerged badger cubs, if you are lucky enough to know where the setts are placed. Go there in the late evening and make sure that you choose a position with the wind blowing towards you, not away from you and towards the badgers. You may see the sow bringing her cubs out, perhaps for the first time. They are charming, playful small animals. Though born in January or February, they do not emerge from the sett until they are about eight weeks old. Even at this age they have the striking black and white faces.

Possibly the great attraction of badger watching is the fact that they are so rarely seen. They have been described as the oldest landowners in Britain. They belong to the musk gland, scent-bearing group of animals which includes stoats, weasels, pine martins and the elusive otters. The earliest form of these family groups was very similar but, during the centuries, they have gradually adapted to different forms of life. The badger has become an excellent digger. Its short but very strong legs can work in very small spaces and the five claws on each foot are long, especially the front ones which are used for digging.

The thrush is a fine singer and a very good parent, and produces very attractive eggs.

A large underground barrow system consists of several chambers where the badger sleeps and breeds. There are possibly several smaller ones. Networks of tunnels link them all. The badger is an extremely clean animal and will line its sett with a mass of dried grasses and straws. In the early spring it rakes this out completely and remakes the whole thing. One can sometimes see piles of straw and grasses, possibly mixed with the grey hairs of the badgers. This will give a clue to whether a sett is being used. If there are barbed wire fences nearby, perhaps you can find several hairs caught there. They are very faithful to certain paths year after year, so one can often see trails that lead to a badger's sett. If the weather has been wet, one can often find their big spread footprints in the mud.

Elder trees will often be seen near a sett, because badgers eat the berries, which pass through their gut and are deposited in the droppings near the sett. Badgers do not have any enemies except man: gamekeepers and farmers are its main persecutors. In the old days they were also baited with dogs, a disgusting activity which is thankfully now a punishable offence.

Badgers do not have very good eyesight and I suggest that if you want to watch them you come on a very quiet evening, bringing some scraps of meat if possible. Set the meat outside the sett and retreat to a not too distant bush, and be still for quite a while. If you are lucky, you will be rewarded with a sight that you will always remember and will want to see again and again.

Hedgerow haven

Quite early in April the hedgerows will clothe themselves in lovely white blossoms. The blackthorn comes out first, whilst the leaves are still closed. Then come the hawthorn flowers, having waited until its green leaves are

Elusive but much liked, badgers are quite plentiful in our region, and are excellent parents.

27

It is a welcome sight to see the skylark feeding its young.
A brown owl enjoys the April sunlight.

unfurled. The long hedgerows are as though covered in snow! At their bottom, you may find the strange form of arum lilies or the tiny blue blossoms of the speedwell, a shy beauty. One of my favourites is the stitchwort, whose star-like flowers are pure white. They have the most delicate of stems and have to rely on pushing through tall grasses or the base of the hawthorns. Since medieval days this little plant has been used as a herb or wort to relieve the stitch or pain in the side - hence its name. The narrow, grass-like leaves were sought-after by pregnant women who believed that eating them would ensure the birth of a boy.

The hedgerow is a world of its own. It provides a welcome shelter along which reptiles, mammals, insects and birds can move without exposing themselves too much to the open fields. It is a silent world during the daytime and we rarely see any movement but during the night it becomes a highway, constantly on the move. It is then that the owls reap the harvest of the night, although the barn owl - sadly decreasing in numbers - will hunt along the verges during the daylight hours. They need a great area to fly over if they are to find sufficient food.

Our pagan ancestors regarded the hawthorn, with all its spikes and gritty, offensive appearance, as a woodland god. During Mayday the leaves were collected whilst the dew remained on them by couples who had spent the night outdoors. The green boughs were brought into their home to bring good luck and fertility. Both the hawthorn and the blackthorn come into their own in the autumn: the hawthorns' millions of red berries are valuable food for the birds, and the blackthorns' sloes will make a quite delicious sloe gin, if one has the patience to pick them and prick them.

Changes afoot in farming

The world of farming is in a state of confused flux. The income of an East Anglian farmer, I should assume, is not as low as it is in many other places, especially in the north of England. Farmers are begged and urged to diversify in every possible way they can but it is something that cannot happen in two minutes, and is very difficult for a man who has been used to a normal farming life all his working days.

I have a very good farming friend in Cumbria, Sir Donald Curry, who has fought vigorously and with great common sense to secure the future of farming. In a Policy Commission on the Future of Food and Farming he urges that organic farmers be able to compete on a level playing field. We could do with far greater numbers of men like him, of vision and ability, controlling the future of our farming industry. What we have now are men and women in government who seem to have no understanding of country ways whatsoever. Mostly brought up in towns, knowing little of country life, and in the stifled atmosphere of Whitehall offices what can they know or understand about the thoughts or directions of people who have been brought up in the country?

I often think of the great change that has come about in the country since I myself was sent out to learn the ways of nature as a small child. A way of life that was heart-warming in its simplicity has evolved to a complex one where we rely almost entirely on machines and computers, the internet and web sites, to govern our lives and those of our children - who seem to understand these machines far better than we adults!

In April nothing is certain. One day there will be sun and the next cold winds and showers. But everywhere there is new growth, a fresh smell and a kind of magic in the atmosphere.

A rare sight now is the red squirrel among the primroses.
Such scenes as this old farm we must try to preserve.

29

May

There is nothing quite so lovely as a bluebell wood on a May morning. The trees that have been bare for months, pushing up their skeletal fingers into the grey skies, are now covered with fresh green. Suspicious of the weather, the ash is the last to come into leaf, and one of the first to drop its leaves in the autumn. The apple orchards and cherry trees are awash now with pink and white blossom. The warmth for which we have waited all winter is back.

The delicate scent and profusion of colourful flowers is all around. We hear the voices of the birds that have migrated to our coasts and countryside for the summer. The song of the blackbird, the song thrush, the willow warbler and a host of others fill the air. We have a pair of song thrushes in our garden and I was able to film them feeding their young during May, amongst the twining stems of the honeysuckle. There has been a drastic decline in the number of thrushes in recent years so I feel privileged to have them so near.

One of the loveliest birds is the bluetit. Now that the small green caterpillars are out in great numbers on the leaves of the trees, the bluetits have their youngsters. In nests and nest boxes they make their soft homes and lay tiny white, brown-spotted eggs. However large the bluetit's family when it hatches, it is gradually whittled down to just one or two which survive into the next year. There is something infinitely cheerful about the bluetit. His little blue cap and yellow plumage reminds me of a schoolboy with his cap and scarf, full of life.

During the winter months we had a diminutive little wren in our garden all by himself, darting about picking up morsels to eat and surviving even the coldest days. The thick of the ivy offered its protection for the night, or perhaps a nest box. The little wren was always with us, and always alone. Now the warm days are here, a pair of them will make one of the loveliest nests in a hole in a tree or behind the ivy, its beautiful dome full of soft mosses in which it can lay its small eggs.

The apple orchards

Is there anything to compare with the beauty and peace of an apple orchard in May? Tragically, in the past few years the great apple orchards of England, and Norfolk in particular, have declined drastically. Prices have been very poor for the growers, with the supermarkets importing from all over the world, though these imported apples rarely compare in quality and taste with our homegrown varieties.

At its height, the Norfolk Fruit Growers Association had 120 members but now there are only 18 growers. The industry was in terminal decline. Trees were ripped up from the orchards, almost halving the area given over to fruit trees - and especially apple trees - within 15 years. The Association's members were staring bankruptcy in the

Right: *Bluebell wood on a May morning.*

A most charming sight to see young bluetits on a May morning.

face. One of the very sensible ideas they came up with was to put aside a large proportion - about a third - of the apple crop for juice to be sold as Norfolk Apple Juice. By September 2001 the now-familiar green bottles were to be found in the shops where we can choose Cox, Russet or Bramley - or opt for a dry, medium or sweet blend of varieties such as Ida Red, Greensleeves and Jonagold. The success of the venture has saved many hundreds of acres of apple orchards, and the livelihoods of the growers.

Conserving the woodland

In Norfolk and Suffolk we benefit greatly from the work of the Woodland Trust. The Trust owns over 1,000 woods covering more than 44,000 acres and has planted over two million trees in recent years. They tell me that since 1930, 50 per cent of this country's ancient woodland has been lost, mainly through conversion to conifer plantation and clearance for agriculture and development. The Trust receives hundreds of calls each year informing them of woods in danger. Ancient woodland is a rich wildlife habitat. Once-common species such as the bluebell, dormouse and the stag beetle are now endangered because their habitat has been reduced to small isolated pockets.

The farmers carry a great responsibility for conserving what woodland we now have left, as they do with the hedgerows and their margins. In this region perhaps more than any other, we have seen hedgerows ripped out

Water lilies will give immense pleasure and colour to any garden.

in the interests of larger fields and more economic production. Thankfully, it is a trend which is beginning to reverse. New hedgerows are being planted. Farmers are beginning to realise the advantages for wildlife of leaving very wide margins alongside the hedgerows - as they used to in the days of the horse and plough. From a very small boy, I have known and admired hedgerow cuttings and the hedgerows themselves. The Norfolk Wildlife Trust is a champion too, pointing out that "In wildlife terms, hedges are like linear woodland, forming important links and corridors of habitat and providing food and shelter where no other may be available. They provide important refuge for many plants and animals and their wildlife is further enhanced if there is an adjacent ditch, verge or field margin present."

In North Norfolk, the great plantings that took place after the Enclosure Acts of 1750 and 1850 and which now characteristically contain more hawthorn and blackthorn than anything else, form a very orderly pattern in the landscape. It is a well-known fact that the great destruction of the hedges began after World War II when every acre was needed to grow for the nation. Since then, over 150,000 miles of hedgerows have been destroyed in this country. Today many hedges are being planted again, consisting purely of hawthorn, which makes a very good but not stock-proof hedge.

As a small boy, I remember watching the hedge-cutters. They went slowly, carefully and methodically along the hedges, cutting them to a real plan that conserved and strengthened them. This was very good for the wildlife.

Hedges should be cut on a two or three year rotation. This work was always carried out in the late winter when work on the farm was quieter.

The charm of butterflies

I often feel when I go out on a beautiful day in May that the world has no greater marvel than a butterfly. It is hard to believe that an egg laid under, perhaps, a stinging nettle leaf can develop into a tiny caterpillar — which in May time is eagerly taken by every bluetit in sight to feed its young — then into a hard-shelled crysallis and finally into an absolute perfection of beauty, the full-blown butterfly. Butterflies have tiny scales, like the tiles of a house, covering their wings and creating their lovely colours.

The largest of our butterflies is the beautiful Swallowtail, which roams around the whole of Europe and even up into the Himalayas, at considerable heights. It is found now with us in the Norfolk Broads and to see it in the reed beds of Hickling Broad is one of the sights which draws many visitors in the summertime. I remember on a remote, lonely island called the Blue Virgin Island off the coast of Sweden, which had not been explored for some 250 years since the time of Lineaus, the Swedish botanist and naturalist, finding one of these beautiful Swallowtails on some cranesbill plants.

Around a pool one can usually find pied wagtails feeding. The majestic swallowtail, only found now in our region.

The butterflies most often seen are the little Orange Tit which comes out very early; the Yellow Brimstone butterfly which can hibernate all the winter in some shed far away from humans; the small Tortoiseshell which also hibernates for the winter; the lovely Comma butterfly which comes from France for the summer, the Peacock with its large eyes on the wings, and - the one I admire most - the Red Admiral. There are also the beautiful little blues and a whole range of fritillaries.

It is a magical world and one wonders at the miraculous change that has come about from the time it was inhabited by those great creatures, the dinosaurs. To stand watching a butterfly break out of its crysallis prison into a world of sunlight and fresh air, it is to marvel at the metamorphosis of such a creature. The wings are at first limp and damp and the butterfly has to wait some time, perhaps two hours, before they dry and become the delicate wings which carry it through storms and wind as well as sunny days until it lays its eggs and then dies.

The Victorians were great collectors of birds' eggs and butterflies. This is, of course, now prohibited. It runs against all our feelings today to net and stick pins through butterflies, as the Victorians did, but I can understand their fascination. There is nothing more beautiful than the sight of butterflies in woodland rides or along the hedgerows on a May morning. There is an old saying about "Can I ever see a thing as lovely as a tree?" The countryside would indeed be bleak and miserable without trees. But it would also be tragic if we did not have these tiny delicate creatures which survive only until their purpose in life - the creation of the next generation - is finished.

One of the most well hidden and attractive nests is that of the willow warbler.

Difficult to capture is this family portrait.

June

The lovely month of June is named after Juno, the wife of Jupiter, and is called the Queen of months. The creamy white blossom is on the dogwood and the elder, a sign that summer is with us. There is a quiet reflective pleasure in the meandering rivers and streams. It is now that we see little wild roses, dog roses, in the hedgerows, and honeysuckle in profusion, many kinds of daisies and grasses, and the fragrant smelling meadow sweet.

There are more than a dozen different species of wild rose in England. The commonest are the dog rose and the field rose. The field rose scrambles about much more than the dog rose, but they both have a lovely perfume given off by the stamens. The white clusters of the elder flower also have a strong, heady scent, a musty perfume that matches the beauty of a June day. Old farm carts were drawn by horses with sprays of elder flowers attached to keep off the flies. In northern Europe there was an old belief that if the flowers were put in ale and a man and woman drank it together they would be married within the year.

The elms and the oaks cast heavy shadows over leaf-bound lanes. Unfortunately, the English elm was almost wiped out in the latter part of the last century but it has not entirely disappeared. Efforts are now being made to plant new trees resistant to Dutch elm disease, which so decimated the population.

The 11th has always been thought of as the start of the haymaking. The 15th is the feast of St. Vitus who is the protector of epileptics. There is a saying that 'If St. Vitus Day be rainy weather, it will rain for forty days together.'

Midsummer Day falls on the 24th June. There are many customs connected with the day. On this day when the sun is at its very highest, the Celts would light huge bonfires in honour of the 'Sun God'.

The red fox

If we are lucky we may glimpse young fox cubs or young badgers playing in the fields and hedgerows near their dens or setts. The fox is very careful, as a rule, to keep out of sight of humans, though often now in urban areas in the winter months they can be seen scavenging for food from bins and on rubbish tips. In Norfolk and Suffolk, however, the fox and the badger can still live a more dignified life in the wide countryside. The red fox is one of the most widespread of all animals, found as far north as the Arctic and throughout Asia, over much of North America and into North Africa. It is not a big animal, often little larger than many domestic cats, though it has a long bushy tail and can weigh about ten kilos. Foxes are most active at dusk and at night but one can, if lucky, watch one in the daylight hours across the fields. They spend most of the year as solitary animals and, unlike

Right: *Fox cubs*

HUGH BRANDON-COX

Tawny owl

Avocets

badgers, have no big family connection. They have a very powerful odour, emitted from glands to define their territory. They do not often start a burrow themselves but instead make use of disused rabbit warrens or parts of badger setts, adding a few pieces of grass or litter. The badger, by contrast, builds a beautifully clean and compact nest in which to shelter its young.

In the breeding season, early in the year, the vixens take over these holes and have four or five young. During the winter months you may hear the high-pitched bark or scream of the red fox as it calls for a prospective mate at night. It is a weird, shrill call, quite frightening. The cubs are very small, blind and dark-furred when born. For the first three weeks, the vixen will not leave them at all. The dog fox brings food to her and is a devoted mate and father. If you know where a fox has its lair, settle yourself one early evening in sight of the den. The youngsters may come out and play with plenty of energy and mock fights, tumbling and falling about under the watchful eye of the vixen, who is constantly on guard. At a hint of danger from man or other animal, she will take each cub by the scruff of the neck and move it to a new hiding place. Foxes are alert to every movement and have wonderful eyesight and a keen sense of smell. So make sure that the wind is blowing from them to you, so that your own scent is not taken to the foxes.

Of course, foxes love rabbits and will go to great lengths to catch them. If the supply of rabbits fails, however, they will eat a wide variety of food. They like mice and voles and will even take insects and worms. Like badgers, foxes also eat a great deal of plant food, as well as carrion such as sheep placenta and stillborn lambs. One thing that annoys the farmer, perhaps more than anything else, is if a fox gets into a hen-house. The sheer fright of the chickens, with their flapping and screaming, seems to make the fox crazy and, as if trying to stop it, he nips the necks of all the chickens in the shed.

Water birds

On the coast, the seabirds are nesting around such places as Blakeney Point and Halvergate Island. You can find the avocets, oystercatchers, plovers, terns, little terns - all those who make their nests on and near the beach. I have watched the young oystercatcher chicks, at the sign or call of danger from their parents, squat down beside a rock and be near-invisible. There they remain until they get the 'all clear' call.

On the ponds and streams, you will see the mallard, or wild duck, with their brood of youngsters going into the water and dabbling for food. At the slightest sign of danger they dive under the water and hide until a reassuring cry from their mother tells them that all is well. When the sun sets and the evening light is soft, the adult birds are more active, searching for frogs, snails, worms and slugs. In the hedgerow ditches, they will look for grain and berries. But despite these wanderings in the fields, their diet mainly consists of aquatic plants from the stream bed, which the mallard reaches by up-tipping, as the swan does.

Flight of swans captured in their beauty.

The male mallard has a lovely deep bottle green head, chestnut breast and creamy white under parts. But these lovely colours disappear in June as the bird moults and is forced to skulk in the reeds for a time. Mallard ducks build a nest lined with soft down, hidden in the reeds or long grasses. The female is very reluctant to ever leave the nest when she is brooding. Together with the mute swans, moorhens, coots and great crested grebes, the mallards are seen with their youngsters trailing behind like bobbing corks.

Pond life

The village pond has been the centre of many English villages since ancient times. Many ponds in Norfolk date

Red and fallow deer can be glimpsed in the woods in early morning or late evening.

back to between 1700 and 1850 when they were dug as marl pits. The marl was spread on the land to reduce acidity in badly drained soils. Clay was also dug for use as a building material in seventeenth century Norfolk, creating ponds. The clay was watered, trodden to mix in short straws and made into blocks, which were left to dry for several days. They were the basis of many a cottage and farmhouse. Today, many of the pits and ponds form important habitats for wildlife and are being carefully cleared and replenished in an effort to preserve them.

On June days, the skylark can be heard high overhead and at night - if you are lucky - the glorious notes of the nightingale. As sunset approaches the air can be filled with the flittering of the pipstrelle and larger bats, out for their evening hunt for insects. The finer the day, the lower the bat's hunt. These little animals have astonishing radar, which identifies any object and bounces back, allowing the bat to avoid anything it is not chasing.

Once the dusk has darkened to night, the moon is 'Mistress of the Night'. There is probably nothing so serenely beautiful as a night when the moon is full and one can watch it over water. Much has been written about the moon and its phases, as it waxes and wanes through the month. The full moon is a time of great pleasure to many people, and yet I have known it when I have laid out under such a moon with shrapnel falling around me and wished that it was a night of great blackness. We speak of the Easter moon, the Harvest moon - one of the loveliest as it hangs low over the ripe cornfields, the Hunter's moon - which follows in September and is also very large, and the Honeymoon - the full moon of love at the time of marriage. Nature, too, reacts to the fullness of the moon. The small mammals find it easier to hunt, as do the owls which can locate mammals even more clearly by its rays.

Right: One of Norfolk's most attractive but secretive creatures, the badger, can be best seen at night.

BADGERS

HUGH BRANDON-YOX

July

The drowsy days of July see the foxgloves at their very best. They prefer the hedgerows around wetlands, attracting the bees to their ever-open blooms. The flowers of the dog rose bloom throughout July and into early August, their white and pale pink flowers giving a lingering fragrance on the soft air. The peacock butterfly, surely one of our loveliest, hovers on the wing.

On a damp misty morning over the meadows and rivers of Norfolk and Suffolk, one can hear and see swallows darting for insects. One delights in their cries as they speed through the air with tremendous agility. Long curved wings allow them to change direction amazingly fast - in fact, at as much as 80 miles per hour - as they pursue insects in the air.

The swallows spend most of their time, as do the swifts, on the wing and capture their prey with a wide gaping mouth. Swallows only come to the ground for collecting mud, which they use for nest building. The nests are skilful works of art, with the weave and mud pellets made entirely with their beaks. On the ground, swallows are terribly awkward. They shuffle along on very small legs and feet. Seeing them, one might think that a swallow is incapable of gaining enough momentum to take to the skies once again, but they do. The birds are about seven inches long with pure white under parts. They have a distinctive red chin, not easily noticed when they are in flight, and a lovely deeply forked tail. They drink from the surface of water whilst flying and then ascend to a considerable height to roost on the wing.

Swallows spend a long winter to the south of the Sahara desert. It was once thought that all swallows from a district submerged themselves together into the mud of a mere, lake or pond for the winter, arising in the following spring. It is estimated, in fact, that they fly a quarter of a million miles - four and a half trips to the moon and back - during a lifetime of migration to and from Africa. In early May we see the first of them come here. By some uncanny sense, of which we know very little, each bird returns to the same barn or nesting place below the eves of a farm house, year after year.

Swallows lay two clutches of eggs and both partners will incubate them. The creamy white, rust-speckled eggs are hidden from sight in the nest. The young ones take their first flights in July and soon the whole family will be sitting along side one another, demanding to be fed and flapping their wings whilst the parents fly back and forth feeding them with insects as fast as they are able. The fact that swallows and house martins feed on flies, which can spread mastitis, has led to the old superstitious thinking that if the farmer destroys a swallow's nest his cows will yield bloody milk.

Right: Great crested grebes are a very colourful sight on the pools and rivers.

Wrens in summer

View to Salthouse

Poppyland

Though considered by many to be a troublesome weed, the scarlet poppy is a wonderful sight. On the north Norfolk coast near Cromer you can see field upon field waving in the breeze. These annual flowers grow in profusion on unfertilised fields. They are not a native plant of England, but are always found on land that has been cultivated or disturbed. Where the poppies lived before farms and fields existed is a mystery to me!

Archeologists have found poppy seeds mixed with ancient barley grains in Egypt and estimate that they are some 3,500 years old. The poppy has long been used by man. Syrup used to be extracted from the petals and oil has been used for cooking and in the preparation of paints. The pale lilac poppy - the opium poppy - has been grown in gardens since the Bronze Age. There are actually eight species of poppy, five of which are found as arable weeds. Poppy flowers have no nectar but their pollen is protein rich. It is collected by bees as food for the young larvae. At the slightest breeze the seeds shake out through perforations in and around the capsule.

The field poppy comes into its own on the November 11, Remembrance Day, when we remember those who gave their lives in the Great War by wearing poppies in our buttonholes. In the battlefields of Flanders, the poppy became so numerous - and symbolic of the lives that were lost - because the shells caused enormous disturbance of the earth. The germination of millions of poppy seeds turned the land, which might otherwise have been bare, into a sea of red.

In July we see many kinds of arable weed - especially in those fields where the farmer leaves a margin between his crops and the hedgerow. One of the most irritating plants is the broad-leafed dock. By contrast, we see the cheerful bright yellow of the dandelion. The root of the dandelion, dried and cut, makes a passable substitute for coffee. The scentless mayweed is found on the coastal shingle and cliffs of Norfolk and Suffolk. It has fleshier leaves than the varieties that grow in fields of crops.

Traditional building skills

In the villages of Norfolk and Suffolk, we still see many thatched cottages and a good many of these are thatched with the famous Norfolk reed. The great reed beds at Cley in Norfolk and on the Broads are the source of much of the reed. You can see the marshmen cutting and bundling the reed for delivery to the thatchers, whose skill is still much in demand. Thatch was extensively used on country cottages, which were constructed of wattle and daub, or clay and straw mixed together, and would have been unable to support very heavy stone tiles. Thatch needs only quite a light framework of battens across the rafters and, by comparison with tiles, is quite light. Today, Norfolk reed is also being used to make fence panels which will last for up to twenty years. The waste reed is chopped up and sold for garden mulch.

From the ancient flint mines and from the seashore itself has come another very popular method of building in our region. Flint is extremely attractive when it is knapped, or split open to display the inside, which is shiny. Houses built of flint and brick look very imposing and solid. Of all building stones, flint has probably been most used across the whole of the chalk belt, from Norfolk to Dorset. With the arrival of bricks, flint became the stone for the less well off and was often used for farm buildings. But in North Norfolk especially, the combination of brick and flint has continued and is still being used today. Many of our churches have knapped flint and have survived many centuries of harsh weather.

There is great appeal about the sight of a pied flycatcher in an ancient oak at this time.

Importance of a climate

We have a tremendous change in the number and variety of birds that come and go in this small island of ours. Seven thousand years ago the Straits of Dover were formed, cutting off the British Isles from Europe and it is against that background that our species of birds are so variable. I will mention one or two birds that I particularly like.

You will see from the illustration on page 45 the lovely pied flycatcher (this is the female) among the oak trees. This kind of bird would normally not have been here - but distance is so little object to birds.

Another bird of which I am particularly fond, is the whinchat. It is often seen on farmland, of which we have much in Norfolk and Suffolk. They can be found, and I have filmed and photographed them, in a nest on the ground hidden by tall thistles and grasses. I have been in a hide and watched them for some time as they are bringing up youngsters and have noticed that they love a tall plant like a meadow sweet to perch on before coming down to the nest.

The whinchat are among the earliest of our summer visitors, starting to arrive here in small numbers in April, journeying right across the Sahara Desert and arriving with the wheatears, yellow wagtails and so on. We should never normally see any of these birds if it were not for this annual migration, from warmer to cooler, and then cooler to warmer breeding grounds.

The whinchat is a near relative of the stonechat, another pretty little bird, you can find on the heath all the year around. I remember in the middle of winter finding one on the top of a gorse bush, which is where they like to be. Once they were very common throughout Britain but now they are very localised in their appearances.

Perhaps, with luck, you may see a whinchat swaying in the breeze on a meadow sweet.

We have an amazing variety of lovely little birds, all called warblers: the whitethroats, the blackcap, the garden warbler, the chiff-chaff and the willow warbler - which has always been one of my favourites - and the grasshopper warbler.   There is even one which is not recorded in England until 1961 and didn't breed until 1973. It is called the cettis warbler, pronounced 'chetty'.   As well as having highly coloured eggs and a very, very powerful song - probably the most powerful of all of them - the males are about 30 per cent heavier than the females, which is very unusual.

Ever-open mouths in the nest of the whinchat in the tall undergrowth.

The mill at Burnham Overy.

47

August

An article I wrote several years ago, Joys of the Countryside, is beginning to pale into insignificance compared with what we now hear on the radio and television about the changing climate of our planet. The world is now, we are told, warming up. The increase in temperature is not very much in a year but when accumulated over several decades the effect is significant.

The tiny, cheeky little blue tits, for whom I have a great affection, have already nested and today they still have the possibility of hatching at a time when the green caterpillars on which they feed are in great abundance (in May). But even now they are later than they used to be. The whole cycle of nature is taking a turn that you would not notice over one or two, or even five years. But in the longer term the world is becoming steadily a warmer place and more and more polluted in the atmosphere.

Still waters

Throughout my own life, I have derived great joy and pleasure from successfully taking some film or still pictures of a pair of birds feeding their rapidly growing youngsters. It is an added pleasure if they come to one's own garden and decide that 'this is the place I want to be for the summer'. In this connection the pond plays an important role. One can have even a tiny pond in the garden and it is still worth having. Thousands upon thousands of men look forward with interest and excitement to sitting by the water, even though they know that if they catch a fish they must put it back. They are amongst the most likely to see the most precious, glorious splash of blue and many other mixed colours in the glory of a dashing kingfisher.

There are two other birds, both with quite a strong voice, which might be glimpsed near the water. You may be in deep reverie and then suddenly the cheerful call of the chaffinch is heard. Chaffinches frequent the garden more and more every year and they seem to have made a fairly good job of surviving over the past few years. The photograph on page 52 shows the full beauty of the nest a chaffinch can make. With no tools to use except beak and claws, the nest can present the appearance of just a ball of moss caught up in the tree but the inside of the nest is lovely, and the eggs seem to blend in so well with all their mottled colours.

The pied wagtail is also a handsome bird with its black and white tail constantly bobbing up and down. It has a great love of the river, where it obtains its food and materials to make its nest. If there is an old barn near you, you will probably find its nest under the eaves there, because it is a favourite spot.

Right: *More and more rare become these small glimpses of harvest mice in summer.*

Pied wagtail

Summer days by the sea

In Norfolk and Suffolk we have stretches of sandy beaches, dunes and heather amongst the best in the country. Tens of thousands come here in the high summer attracted by the historic timbered towns and villages, the unspoilt countryside and coastline and the wildlife reserves such as Minsmere, Titchwell, Hickling, Strumpshaw and Cley Marshes.

I often go to Morston on the Norfolk coast for a period of calm relaxation. From there you can see Blakeney Point and the boats going on every tide, filled with visitors, to see the grey and common seals on the sand banks near the Point, or onto the Point itself to see wild birds. I have painted several pictures called 'Waiting for the Boat', the rows of people a colourful sight as they stand patiently until the tide is right to clamber into the boats that take them to the sandbanks, a round trip of a couple of hours.

The growing interest in wildlife, conservation and country matters in general is a trend to be welcomed, in spite of the dangers of increasing numbers of people visiting some sites. In Norfolk and Suffolk we welcome the visitors with open arms whilst also trying to ensure that the natural habitat and environment remains unspoilt. Most encouraging is the tremendous interest amongst young people, and the efforts to help them learn in a stimulating way. Few of us have not, as small children, enjoyed warm summer days with nets and lines, poking around rocky pools on the beach. There are all sorts of tiny creatures, a

Life feels wonderful on an August day by a bubbling stream.

miniature world to be explored. I remember when I was young being fascinated by many kinds of seaweed. In those days, several of the daily newspapers had summertime competitions about the beach. I would go down to the beach on a Friday evening and Saturday morning, collecting seaweed and building sandcastles - and won my first big nature book this way.

It was in my youth too that I developed a great fondness for piers. It was August 1923 when, as a very small boy, I joined my grandmother and her five vivacious daughters for a trip by carriage to the small town of Clacton. Today, I have the same feeling for Cromer Pier. Piers have a charm that is hard to convey. Walk the length of a pier and gaze back at the town. Watch the water rushing in

between the strong supporting legs, and the shining sand and mud. Somehow you feel a little different and more adventurous than when you stand on firm land.

Motorway riches

When we travel to our holiday destinations by car, perhaps along the motorways, we should remember that these great roads (which have cut a swathe through much of our countryside, though thankfully less so in Norfolk) are also the saviour of many birds and small mammals.

A very long-sighted Transport Ministry has planted literally millions of trees and shrubs along the motorways. Some 57 species of grasses, plants and trees have all

Black and white woodpeckers have amazing strength in their sharp beaks.

To make a garden even better a pair of chaffinches perhaps will have built an exquisite nest in the fork of a tree.

helped to create one of the best shelters for wildlife. It helps also to soften some of the noise of the traffic and to lessen the effects of air pollution. Less visible from the car but no less important are the drainage ditches that have been dug. Some of them are filled with water all the year round and are a wonderful fresh water habitat for many species. It is said that about a quarter of all the 2,000 or so British wildflowers and a third of our grasses are to be found on motorway verges. In places along Norwich's Southern Bypass, cowslips can be seen in tens of thousands, waves of pale yellow nodding heads. Dandelions, campions, hogweeds and oxeye daisies are to be seen.

The advent of major roads and the massive increase in car ownership has, of course, changed the nature of the countryside - even in Norfolk which has traditionally been a 'land apart'. Writing in the 1940s, J. Wentworth Day called Norfolk 'The most English corner of all England'. He added,

> 'If the rest of England were to sink suddenly and Norfolk be left alone in the cold waters of the North Sea it would not, I think, bother itself unduly for Norfolk is the most individual county in all England. It is almost self-contained, magnificently proud and owes little to outside sources and supply. It is ancient and historic yet up-to-date and energetic in the true essentials of good and simple living. It is, in fact, England in little. Or perhaps I should say old England in little. That is true of East Anglia as a whole.'

Right: *Waiting for the boat at Morston.*

September

A thick mist hangs over the river Bure as I walk along the bank. It is early morning, in the first days of September. The silence is broken by the hoarse, raucous cry of a cock pheasant as it speeds off into the undergrowth. In the shadows I glimpse an old grey heron, suddenly rising with a gasping, rasping cry to disappear into the mist.

On just such a morning, with the pale light shining through my window, I have heard an eerie, piercing screech as the grey shadow of a barn owl has crossed the field in front of me, in pursuit of a mouse or some other small rodent. This is one of the loveliest birds and, sadly, one in decline. They favour rough grassland and open landscapes with scattered trees, where they can perch and watch for their quarry. The barn owl needs more of the wide verges that used to exist around every field when the ploughs were drawn by horses which needed the space to turn. And, these days, many of the barns which used to offer roosting and nesting places for the owls have been made into homes. But, fortunately, as farmers become more aware of the plight of our bird life, they are taking measures to help. Some are erecting big boxes for the owls, from which they can swoop down to catch rats and other rodents. They have wonderful eyesight and hearing which enables them to hunt down rodents even on bright, sunny days and to detect the smallest of movements through the grass.

As a boy I reared two tawny owls which became fascinating friends and would perch on my shoulder, perfectly free to come and go in the countryside. They had the most beautiful, luminous eyes which seemed almost to offer a gateway to their souls. They are, of course, quite unlike the barn owl, which has the fierce, aggressive eyes of a hunter.

A sudden whirring of down-curved wings catches my eye as a small covey of grey partridges rise and then disappear over a hedge. These birds were once very numerous but over-shooting reduced their numbers drastically some 200 years ago and the handsome French partridge was introduced here, though these too are now a rarity. The pheasant, on the other hand, seems to be doing very well in the part of Norfolk where I live. Handsome male pheasants stride about here in the autumn sun as though they owned the place. In fact, we have one that comes into our garden and treats it very much as its own territory.

It is in September that we are most likely to see the colourful little goldfinch on the top of the thistles that are now spreading their seeds. This lovely bird has wings that are mainly black with broad bands of yellow, a red face and the rest of the head black and white. Towards the end of 19th century, the number of goldfinches was brought dangerously low by intensive trapping for the caged-bird trade. In 1860 it was reported that 132,000

Right: *Barn owl*

HUGH BRANDON-COX

were caught in Worthing, in Sussex. The Society for the Protection of Birds made the saving of the goldfinch from trapping one of its first priorities. Of course, changes in agricultural practice have reduced the thistle heads among which it feeds, though they still grow where the land is uncultivated. Another very attractive bird, again almost too brilliant to be English, is the bullfinch, with its pink breast, black head and grey back. They are disliked intensely by the apple growers for they nip the fruit trees when they are in bud, with their springy, short rounded beak. The blackbirds too are fond of ripened apples and, of course, so are the wasps.

Fragile beauty

Most of the butterflies in England cannot survive our winter and we depend for their appearance on mass migration from their breeding grounds, often in the Mediterranean region. The most regular of the migrants are the Red Admiral, Painted Lady and Clouded Yellow. The lovely Swallowtail, which is now so rare, can only be found in parts of Norfolk, particularly on the Broads.

Early September is the time we are most likely to catch sight of the Red Admiral, often lingering on Michaelmas daisies. Some Red Admirals do hibernate through a British winter if it is not too severe. It is easy to overlook them as they chose inaccessible positions in which to hibernate, for example, high up in the trees, either on exposed trunks or hidden among dead leaves and ivy.

The barn owl is a truly lovely bird.
One of my favourite butterflies is the small tortoiseshell in autumn.

The small Tortoiseshell butterfly is a great one for hibernating during the winter in gardens, cellars and places not too exposed to cold winds. Lured out by a warm, sunny day in the every early spring, they can look very dilapidated. Their fragile wings are damaged by wind, rain and by the wet leaves that brush against them. In these conditions they keep their wings tightly closed and shelter as best they can under the foliage or in dense ivy patches. But usually, when the cold weather comes in

the autumn the butterflies disappear, flying south in the same way as the birds at this time. It seems impossible that these tiny, fragile creatures could move over such long distances, but they do.

Both bird and butterfly delay their departure as long as possible. But they know instinctively that if the weather is unkind, a very dangerous journey lies ahead. For this reason, the goose, the butterfly or the warblier will set off in the protection of a group towards a destination that may be several thousand miles distant.

Beware the ragwort

I have noticed, especially in Suffolk at this time of year, a large amount of ragwort - a yellow plant that is death to many creatures if eaten. Today, landowners are urged very firmly to try to eradicate this yellow weed which causes irreversible liver damage. It is quite deadly to horses, cattle, and sheep - all of which suffer weight loss and a staggering gait followed by blindness, paralysis and death. It is only necessary for an animal to eat about two pounds of ragwort to die. You can find ragwort on roadside verges and fields where no measure has been taken to control it. In recent years it has also started to spread very widely - a single plant can produce 150,000 seeds with a 70 per cent germination rate. This pernicious weed starts to flower in July and continues into September. The advice to all who see ragwort in Norfolk and Suffolk is to dig it out, roots and all.

Standing midway between summer and the real autumn, September can be a tranquil and rather beautiful month. Swallows gather in thousands on the telephone lines, waiting for the day when their instinct tells them to be off for warmer climes. In the countryside the brambles, it seems, had flowers only yesterday. Now they glisten with blackberries to be picked by human hand or hungry bird.

Rookery Farm - the cries of the rooks are one of the delights of the East Anglian scene in September.

Red admiral, a truly lovely butterfly.

October

The smell of dew-soaked fields rises in the early morning mist. Countless leaves of bronze, russet, yellow and gold make this the golden month of October. As I walk the lanes around my home, the pheasants scatter. Soon, they will be caught in the crossfire of guns but for now the cocks remain in their glory and the hens scuttle in the undergrowth of the woodlands, ignorant of the fate that will shortly befall them.

The low-lying mist slowly dispels as the white sun pushes its weak rays through, revealing newly sown fields of winter wheat. Already the green shoots stand erect in thousands of close rows, merging into the misty distance of the far horizon. The land smells at its earthiest best.

October brings an abundance of berries. Purple-hued elderberries hang in large clusters; the scarlet rose hips hold glistening drops of dew. Hawthorn and blackberries offer rich pickings for the birds. Amongst them, etched by the early morning sun, a network of cobwebs has been spun by multitudes of industrious spiders during the night.

The spiders are not alone in their night work. Especially during autumn nights, there is constant movement of birds, animals and insects during the hours of darkness. Some of the most memorable moments of my life have been spent in the open, in the company of, or near proximity to, the wildlife which takes to the trail after dark.

From a very small boy I have been greatly attracted and influenced by the North Star. I used to read myself to sleep with books of the adventurers, the Vikings who came to our shores in the ninth century, finding their way by the light of that North Star. The Lapps too, with whom I was later to travel with their reindeer across frozen wastes, used the star as their guiding light. So do the geese, and other birds that appear almost by magic along our coast, use that same North Star for their great migrations.

I recall an evening on the big mud flats outside Brancaster, thinking about the Vikings - literally, 'men of the creeks' - landing their craft along these northern inlets. It is easy to imagine their high-prowed, square-sailed long boats coming in with the flood tide, their small keels making it possible to sail over very shallow water.

In 850 AD a group from Denmark wintered on this lonely, isolated coast, sharing the open space with the birds. Then in 866 a large force came to seek homes here, bringing many skills with them. They left behind much evidence of their occupation, including many of the place names we use today.

When Norfolk was still joined to the European continent, this was once a land of forests, swamps and fresh water pools. It was inundated with salt water in around 6400 BC. At several points along the coast today, at Titchwell and Thornham, for instance, the trunks and stools of

Right: *A slim, very fierce killer is the stoat.*

HUGH BRANDON-COX

Oystercatchers gather on the shore.
Brent geese return for the winter.

those ancient trees can still be seen at low tide. Man has been around here for thousands of years, making a precarious living from the sea and the land.

October is the time when the geese and the waders return to the north Norfolk and Suffolk coasts in their millions, from their summer nesting places in far-off northern places. I like to recall the days when I followed the midnight trail with the Arctic Nomads. We took ancient trails that led us, with 600 reindeer, to the coast and then over to a small island for the summer months to escape the gadfly and mosquito-ridden mainland. We travelled into the night, on sledges, carrying the poles and canvas which were to be our shelter for rest during the daylight hours. The night sky was like velvet, with the North Star shining bright and clear. Around us, the quiet movement of the deer and swishing of skis carried through the air as the herdsmen moved up and down with their dogs. Out of the stillness came a soft sound, growing louder and louder until it resembled the baying of a pack of hounds on the scent. Against the illumination of the star, a huge flock of pinkfeet geese became visible. They were returning from, perhaps, Snettisham or Brancaster or parts of the Suffolk coast where they had spent the long winter. Back in the far north, they would spread out on the tundra for the nesting season.

The lands of north Norfolk and north Norway have more in common than these migratory birds. The people of both places have lived over the centuries by fishing and cultivation of small plots of land; it has always been a hard existence in sometimes bitter, blinding cold weather.

One of the most colourful and certainly noisiest of all the invading birds is the black and white oystercatcher. They gather in their thousands, especially at Hunstanton. They are the very last birds to leave the roost because they go for the mussel beds that are only exposed at the very low tides. I have a fascination for these birds because I watched them coming from north Norway when I was in my old Lapp hut at the edge of the fjord, and fancied that

I saw the very same birds on my return to Norfolk. Oystercatchers are companionable birds with bright red beaks which are ideal for breaking mussel shells. It is estimated that a single bird can eat up to 100 mussels or 500 cockles a day!

In the countryside too, we see other migratory birds appearing in preparation for the winter. The fieldfares and the redwings arrive from Scandinavia, along with the glittering, many-coloured waxwings. This is the time when fierce gales and storms sweep through the lanes, showering leaves in careless abundance on to the soaked earth below, where they remain to turn slowly into productive goodness for the soil. The remaining apples are blown down with a hard thud as the boughs twist and shake in the gusts. But on the days when wind and rain are at bay, October brings with it a quiet contemplative mood, a time for reflection.

The fight to survive

There is a small jungle in which all the players are playing a game called the fight to survive. Most of the activity of our tiny predators takes place after dark when the world of humans is mostly asleep. One of the animals that I like extremely well is the wood mouse and that, together with the dormouse and the harvest mouse, which are delicately charming and beautiful in their own way, and all the voles and shrews, have to beware of what is really the main enemy at night, the owl.

But during the day there are also two other vicious little predators, very slim and agile, and the enemy of every creature up to the size of a rabbit. I am talking about the stoat and the weasel. In the north, the stoat will change colour sometimes to become white, and is called ermine, for the winter. From this lovely material many coats have been made in the past but now the trade is all stopped. The stoat has a slim body and a black tip to its long tail. It is very inquisitive and sometimes you will see it

Pheasants over the autumn fields.

The great spotted woodpecker.

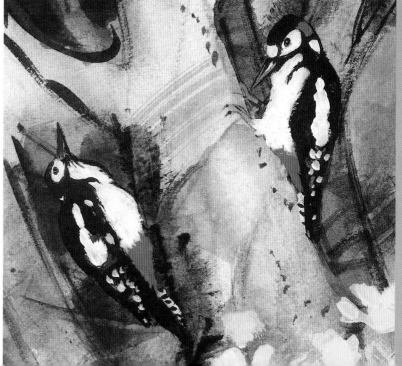

61

Wood mouse

jumping up on its hind legs and peering around. This it does to lure rabbits, in particular. Rabbits seem to be utterly hypnotised by the approach of a stoat and when they are finally trapped they let out a piercing squeal before they die and the agile stoat is left with a body far larger than its own to drag back to its burrow.

The weasel is a similar type of animal, though even smaller. Despite being the smallest of the flesh eating predators, the weasel has tremendous courage and will attack almost anything. Voles, rats and mice, frogs and rabbits, they all fall to the weasel although it is so tiny and very few escape because it can get into the smallest crack between old stone walls and pursue its prey almost anywhere. It has of course a reputation, especially amongst older people, of being the personification of evil.

But there it is. The little stoat and the even smaller weasel both have to kill to survive.

The tapping of the woodpecker

The hedgerows stand starkly naked of all green, except for the ivy which gives shelter to a host of insects. There is little sound in the woods, apart from the harsh tapping of the woodpecker. We have three varieties: the lovely shy Green, the rapid moving, very small Spotted, and the larger Greater Spotted, with its very bold black and white plumage and patches of red for the male.

The large Green, with its bright crimson crown, is a really handsome bird if it can be glimpsed for a moment in the sun on a tall beech. It is so shy that it is rarely seen, but its very loud cry of 'yaffle' has earned it the name of the laughing 'pecker. It enjoys life where older beech and oaks have rotting branches. With its strong beak it pulls off chunks of the wood to reveal the mass of insects that find a home in such surroundings. I have seen it best when it searches for ants in the colonies that can be found in woodlands.

I think we have all seen the round hole of a 'pecker high up in a trunk of beech. Their ability to smash into a tree trunk is remarkable. One would not think it possible for a bird to dig out a nesting site in this fashion, but they are adapted for the task. The young are very noisy in their confined space during the time they are being fed, and it is then that one can more easily find an occupied home.

Enjoy each winter day. It can be as wonderful as we make it in our own thoughts.

The Greater Spotted woodpecker can often be seen at a nesting hole.

63

November

An abiding November memory for me is shivering in a thick 'pea souper' as I waited on the station platform for the train that would take me home. Fortunately, the ban on coal fires in cities has made the so-called smogs of the early and middle twentieth century a thing of the past and the old saying "November - no flowers, no sun, no life" no longer rings so true. Nonetheless, this is a month that can be bleak and miserable, a time when we are thankful for warm fires and other comforts.

Like many small boys, my recollections of November have much to do with Guy Fawkes and Bonfire night. Each year I would make my Guy and, carrying him in a small barrow, would ask for "A penny for the Guy", collecting enough to buy my own fireworks. On those cold, dank evenings I would delight in watching the bonfire sparks rising to the sky and the fireworks explode in a multitude of colours.

But it is not just on Bonfire night that we enjoy a good fire, so it is as well to know that there is great advantage in trying to secure the right wood for it. Some trees make good burning logs, others not so. I would put the ash above all others for fine, split logs and a fragrant smell. When you can get them, pear, cherry and apple are also very good and fine for fragrance. The holly makes another solid log, which can be burnt 'green' and still give off a good flame. When the birds have finished with the berries, the hawthorn also burns very well and produces a fine heat.

When I was in Scandinavia, it was always the silver birch that would be cut and split and stacked into neat piles for the winter. It too gives off a fast and pleasant heat, but it burns very quickly and the log pile soon needs replenishing. Pines are good for burning, especially the larch whose twigs are ideal for starting the fire. The oak is an old reliable, if it is old and dry enough. Then it will burn with a fierce red glow, although it has an acrid edge which one can feel in the throat and eyes.

Beech wood is also a good burner and splits very well because of its straight grain; but it also needs to be well seasoned for, say two or three years. I used to be a great lover of the tall English elms, and painted many in their winter skeletons. Now, sadly, the elm has been all but wiped out by Dutch elm disease and the rooks have had to find refuge in other tall trees such as the oak. On a bitterly cold November morning, look for the rooks gathered like old women from a mining town, their black feathers like shawls around their gaunt frames.

Life is not easy for the birds. Years ago, when threshing was far less efficient than it is today, many birds would feed well at this time of the year from the seeds that were left as corn was threshed out to store in the barns. The fields too, which were not put under the plough so quickly after the harvest, offered a good source of food

Right: *Lapwings*

HUGH BRANDON-COX

well into the winter. Amongst the stubble there was food in plenty for both birds and small mammals. Today there is new seed planted in the fields almost before summer is ended.

In our woodlands and forests, the demand for tidiness and productivity has undermined the natural process of decay and composition. Plants, fungi, insects and animals all depend on decaying matter - just as the soil is enriched by it. Just turn over the earth when you are in woodland and you will smell the mould. There will be millions of bacteria invisible to the naked eye and perhaps the white threads in leaf litter which are the spreading branches of fungi. Just one fifth of the fauna that would have existed in woodland and forest perhaps 100 years ago still exists today. Many of the insects that filled dead and rotting wood - small beetles, wood lice and hundreds of species of fungi - are no longer to be found.

Thankfully, in some conservation areas today, rotting trees are left where they fall, providing sanctuary for bird, insect and animal life. It can take 20 years or so for a large log to reach the final stage of decay, when all the nutrients valuable to the soil have been used up. There are many creatures that colonise rotting trees; some invade the dying trees, to be followed by others that specialise in the final stages of decay. The fauna which inhabit dead wood play a vital part in the forest community, providing food for insect eaters like hedgehogs, shrews and some birds.

The ancient oaks around Norfolk and Suffolk are often riddled with beetle burrows and the holes they make are favourite haunts for bats and owls. We all know about the tapping of the woodpecker but there are many other, less noisy, birds which love the old oaks and other trees. They include the nuthatch, blue tit, pied flycatcher and night owl.

Like all other creatures, the owls must find food to live. Their shrill calls can be heard late into the night, and through to the dawn. The barn owls wing silently among

Typical of November is this dramatic view.
Partridges in flight.

66

the grave stones of country churchyards in search of food - in earlier times giving rise to the belief that they were the spirits of the dead.

In many of those same country churchyards, there still stand venerable yew trees, always looking solemn and melancholy but especially so on grey November days. Yew is certainly one of the most ancient trees and in England we have some of the finest specimens in the whole of Europe. These were the trees that, as a boy, impressed me most. When I was older I started painting tall, umbrella-shaped elms too, till they became quite a symbol of my work. Then came the tragic Dutch elm disease which wiped out almost all, changing much of our traditional countryside. The rooks, which used to nest in their top-most branches, had to seek other habitats - usually the tall oaks and pines which are also favoured by grey herons.

In the dying days of November, as the top branches and twigs of these trees begin to show starkly against the sky, we know that we are in the last of the fall.

Masses of berries and colourful braken are seen in November.

67

December

For some of us, December is a time of great rejoicing, of much pleasure at Christmas time as the family gathers together. For others, it can be a time of great loneliness. In the wilds, it can be both a time of quiet - for hibernation or reflection - and one of noisy activity as the birds sweep in from colder climes.

For all of us, the December days are short. The dawn comes quite late and often fog and mist can obliterate the landscape. The evening darkness falls all too soon. As it does, the rooks gather in noisy formations in the naked trees, wheeling and twisting as they settle down, huddling together to see the long night through.

During the day these and other birds such as the lapwings, are in constant search for food. In doing so, they perform a useful service to the farmers by ridding the land of many of the grubs which threaten their crops. The distinctive-looking lapwing, with its black cap and wispy crest, is a familiar but declining sight in the farmed countryside. It breeds in loose colonies over the fields, gathering into flocks in the winter and roosting in tight groups. The birds can be seen rising from the fields, in V's or irregular masses, circling and returning to the fields.

Big battalions of redwings and fieldfares, and even waxwings, arrive from Scandinavia to spend a milder winter with us. Migrating birds in their hundreds of thousands, if not millions, have by now arrived in Norfolk and Suffolk. Many of them occupy the rich mudflats around the coast. Visit at this time of year and they will be teeming with life - surely a sight worth braving the cold winds of this captivating place.

Even so late in the year, the hawthorn hedges still bear their berries - a life sustaining larder for the birds. The nuthatch is as at home on the ground seeking fallen nuts and berries as it is foraging on the walls of old buildings and in tall trees. These little birds are expert, agile climbers, often hanging head-down as well as perched across a branch, using strong feet and sharp claws to keep their balance. But the nuthatch and many birds, especially the insect-eating ones, need our help to see them through the winter. Clean water, nuts and pieces of fat provide a life line for them, even in relatively mild weather.

The holly and the ivy, those symbols of a traditional Christmas, are welcomed by the birds too. The luscious red berries of the holly are a valued source of food for them - as well as for decorating our halls. The ivy, clinging to walls and trunks of trees, provides shelter for hibernating insects behind its thick leaves during the winter months, as it provided rich supplies of nectar during the late autumn.

As far back as 1444, the association between holly and Christmas time has been recorded: "Every man's house, also the churches, were decked with holly and the conducts in the streets were garnished likewise". Of course, pagan traditions go back well before this time but it was really during Victorian times that the celebration of

Right: *December can often be a very bleak month.*

The search for food - nuthatches, and squirrels.

Christmas took on the traditions we still observe today - most notably the Christmas card and tree.

It is rare now - perhaps because of global warming - that we experience the white Christmas that is so much a part of that tradition. It seems only a few years ago that the ice could be really thick and feasts would be held on lakes and ponds, with roasts cooked over blazing fires. But today Christmas often brings miserable weather, with the odd fortunate exceptions.

I recall a recent Christmas day at Strumpshaw Fen, an RSPB nature reserve near Norwich, and at Buckenham Marshes. We were the only people bumping through the big puddles on the rough track leading down to the river Yare where we parked our car. We were rewarded by the sight of thousands of beautiful wigeon, with their lovely colouring and whistling calls, which had sought out this very special place for their winter home.

My own lifelong interest in the natural world began one Christmas when, as a small boy, my stocking included - along with other small gifts and some apples and oranges - a book about nature. It set me off on a trail though many miles of countryside, in this country and abroad. An early observation was the struggle for survival which faces all insects, birds and animals. All have an instinct for finding and conserving food during hard times. Our hedgerows, now mercifully being replanted rather than destroyed, provide living quarters all the year round for a multitude of small mammals that we rarely see. Among these is the wood mouse, characterised by its very large eyes.

I had the good fortune to watch this little charmer in my garden one autumn, climbing up the stems of red campion to reach the seeds. It was a masterpiece of balance and one I was able to film. The wood mouse depends on finding its food at the bottom of hawthorn bushes and rose bushes, gathering berries and rose hips even into December. Many of them are gathered in and stored, sometimes in a deserted bird's nest. The growth of the wood mouse's teeth is checked only by its constant gnawing to keep them short. The little creature will cover an area of about half a mile from its known territory in search of bulbs, acorns, snails and grain as well as berries and hips.

The wood mouse has a body about three and a half inches in length and a tail as long again. It can bound along in a kangaroo fashion, leaping up to four feet. Sometimes you might be lucky to see their tracks in the snow, appearing larger than you would ever imagine. The little wood mouse is often taken by foxes, owls, birds of prey and even by adder snakes. But survive they do in their precarious way.

In the countryside the muted hues of December are never really drab. There is plenty to catch the eye - not least the bird life. We can watch the redwings and fieldfares as they find rich pickings in the hedgerows. We see them wheeling across the sky in great flocks. There is a silence in the fields, but the buds are already there to be seen, ready to swell and burst into life - a promise of the spring to come.

Resting wigeons - a lovely sight.
Softly wakes the dawn - coots on ice.

Overleaf: *Lonely beauty on a December morning.*